Illustrations by John P Gannon MA

Published by John P Gannon MA

For information:

johnthemobileappmakers@yahoo.co.uk

ISBN:

Printed in USA

# <u>Anxiety</u>

## THE Plague

## OF The Western World

This MANUAL Offers Help And Understanding To Teens

Written and Illustrated

by

John P Gannon MA

# Table of Contents

<u>Introduction to Anxiety</u>

# Chapter 1

## Introduction to Anxiety

## Understanding and Support

In establishing the foundation for comprehending anxiety, this chapter serves as a guiding light, illuminating the path toward a positive and supportive discourse on mental health tailored specifically for teenagers.

# Tips for Dealing with Anxiety

## Deep Breathing:
Practice deep, slow breaths. Inhale deeply through your nose, hold for a few seconds, and exhale slowly through your mouth. This can help activate your body's relaxation response.

## Grounding Techniques:
Focus on your senses to ground yourself in the present moment. Pay attention to what you can see, hear, touch, taste, and smell.

## Mindfulness and Meditation:
Mindfulness practices, such as meditation, can help calm your mind and reduce anxiety. Apps like Headspace or Calm may be helpful.

## Physical Activity:
Regular exercise can positively impact your mood and reduce anxiety. It doesn't have to be intense - even a short walk can be beneficial.

**Limit Stimulants:** Reduce or avoid caffeine and nicotine, as they can contribute to increased feelings of anxiety.

## Adequate Sleep:
Ensure you are getting enough sleep, as lack of sleep can exacerbate anxiety.

## Talk to Someone:
Share your feelings with someone you trust, whether it's a friend, family member, or mental health professional. Talking about your worries can be a relief.

## Set Realistic Goals:
Break down tasks into smaller, more manageable goals. This can help prevent feeling overwhelmed.

## Limit Exposure to Stressors:
Identify and, if possible, limit exposure to sources of stress. This might include setting boundaries with certain activities or people.

# <u>Overview</u>

Anxiety, as a fundamental and adaptive response to stress, is a natural instinct intricately woven into the human experience. It acts as a compass, helping individuals navigate life's challenges. However, when anxiety transcends its adaptive role, persisting and overwhelming, it metamorphoses into the intricate tapestry of an anxiety disorder.

# Types of Anxiety

Navigate the diverse landscape of anxiety disorders, introducing teenagers to the spectrum that encompasses Generalized Anxiety Disorder (GAD), Social Anxiety, and Panic Disorder. Each represents a unique facet of the intricate emotional landscape teenagers may traverse.

# Normalizing Emotions

Embrace the normalcy of occasional anxiety, emphasizing that experiencing stress is an integral part of the human journey. Drawing a clear distinction between the ebb and flow of regular stress and the more enduring nature of clinical anxiety lays the groundwork for understanding when additional support becomes essential.

## Prevalence Among Teenagers

Statistics: Paint a realistic portrait by sharing relevant statistics that underscore the prevalence of anxiety among teenagers. This statistical exploration not only assures readers that they are not alone in their experiences but also validates the collective nature of their struggles.

# Understanding the Numbers

Delve into the contributing factors behind the escalating prevalence of anxiety in today's society. Unpack the intricate web woven by societal expectations, academic pressures, and the omnipresent influence of social media. By doing so, provide readers with a context that enables them to comprehend the multifaceted nature of this pervasive issue.

# Normalizing the Conversation

## Breaking Stigmas

Courageously confront the pervasive stigma enveloping mental health. Emphasize that seeking help is not a testament to weakness but an act of profound courage and self-care. Challenge stereotypes, dismantling barriers, and fostering a paradigm shift towards understanding and empathy.

# Encouraging Openness

Illuminate the paramount importance of open and honest conversations about mental health within families, schools, and communities. Advocate for an environment where the act of discussing emotions is not only accepted but celebrated, cultivating a culture of support and understanding.

# Creating a Supportive Atmosphere

## Safe Spaces

Shed light on the profound significance of safe spaces where teenagers can freely express their emotions without fear of judgment. Whether found at home, in school, or within friendships, these sanctuaries play a pivotal role in nurturing emotional well-being.

## Peer Support

Emphasize the transformative role of peer relationships in creating a supportive environment. Encourage friendships founded on empathy, understanding, and a genuine willingness to lend a compassionate listening ear.

# Providing Practical Advice

## Recognizing Anxiety

Offer practical and tangible guidance on recognizing signs of anxiety, encompassing behavioural, emotional, and physical indicators. Equip readers with the tools to identify when their stress levels may require thoughtful attention.

# <u>Seeking Help</u>

Stress the paramount importance of proactively reaching out for support. Whether from friends, family, or professionals, seeking help is not a sign of vulnerability but a proactive step towards managing anxiety and fostering resilience.

# Resources for Further Support

## Hotlines and Helplines

Illuminate the existence of vital helplines that offer immediate assistance. Instil the knowledge of where to turn in moments of crisis, providing an essential lifeline for readers grappling with urgent emotional challenges.

# Chapter 2

## Causes of Anxiety

## Unveiling the Tapestry of Influences

As we embark on unravelling the intricate web of factors contributing to anxiety, this chapter aims to provide a comprehensive understanding of the diverse elements influencing the development and exacerbation of anxiety in teenagers.

# Examining the Various Factors

## The Complex Nature of Anxiety

Anxiety is a phenomenon of profound complexity, intricately woven into the fabric of human experience. Acknowledge its multifaceted nature, shaped by an interplay of biological, psychological, and environmental factors. This recognition dispels the notion of a one-size-fits-all condition, highlighting the uniqueness of each individual's journey.

Biological Factors: Delve into the genetic blueprint that may predispose individuals to anxiety. Explore the intricate dance of certain genetic traits, acknowledging their role in amplifying susceptibility to anxiety disorders. Shed light on neurotransmitters and their role in mood regulation, unravelling the intricate neurobiological tapestry.

Psychological Factors: Navigate the psychological landscape, exploring personality traits and coping mechanisms. Delve into the impact of past experiences, including traumatic events or adverse childhood experiences, on shaping vulnerability to anxiety. This psychological exploration provides a nuanced understanding of the intricacies at play.

# Environmental Factors

Illuminate the impact of the environment on anxiety. Whether it's the dynamics of family life, socioeconomic status, or cultural influences, each contributes to the intricate mosaic. Address the role of growing up in high-stress environments, acknowledging how these factors can contribute to the development of anxiety disorders.

## Genetics and Inherited Tendencies

Elaborate on the hereditary aspect of anxiety, where certain genetic markers or familial history may heighten the likelihood of developing anxiety disorders. Emphasize that while genetics play a significant role, they do not determine destiny, allowing room for individual agency and resilience.

## Neurobiological Mechanisms

Embark on a journey into the neurobiological underpinnings of anxiety disorders. Illuminate the role of brain structure and function, unveiling the intricate mechanisms at play. Discuss the delicate balance of neurotransmitters like serotonin and dopamine and their contribution to the symphony of anxiety.

# Environmental Stressors

Family Dynamics: Examine the profound influence of family life on anxiety. Discuss how parental relationships, parenting styles, and family support intricately Mold a teenager's mental well-being. Uncover the subtle yet impactful ways in which the family environment contributes to the emotional landscape.

# Sociocultural Factors

Explore the intricate dance between societal expectations, cultural norms, and stress. Delve into the pressure to conform, societal standards of success, and the pervasive influence of social media in shaping perceptions of self-worth. This exploration paints a vivid picture of the societal influences intertwined with the individual experience.

## Academic Pressure

Educational Expectations: Address the pervasive issue of academic pressure. Unpack the stressors related to exams, competition, and the towering expectations placed on teenagers to excel academically. Discuss how these pressures contribute to the onset or exacerbation of anxiety, weaving the academic dimension into the tapestry of causes.

## Balancing Act

Offer insights into achieving a harmonious balance between academic achievement and overall well-being. Encourage a paradigm shift, urging readers to broaden their perspective on success, recognizing that it extends beyond academic performance. This shift in perspective empowers them to navigate the academic land scape with a focus on holistic growth.

By dissecting the causes of anxiety in this chapter, readers are equipped with a nuanced understanding of the multitude of factors shaping their mental landscape. The goal is to empower teenagers to recognize and address these factors, fostering a proactive approach to managing their mental health. The tone resonates with empathy, providing a guiding light as they navigate the intricate tapestry of influences shaping their mental well-being.

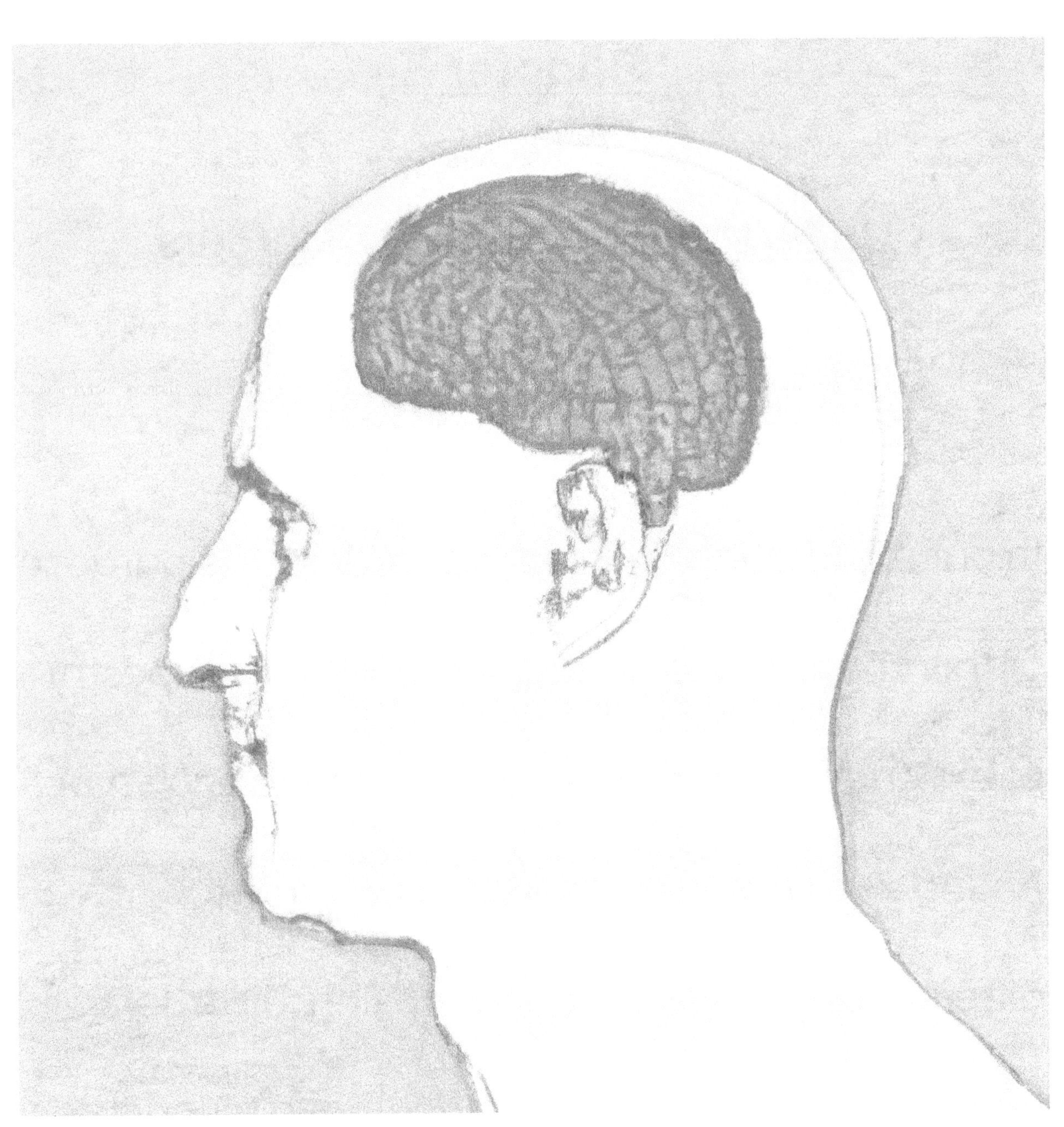

# <u>Understanding Anxiety Disorders</u>

# Chapter 3

## Understanding Anxiety Disorders

## Navigating the Spectrum

In our exploration of anxiety disorders, the purpose of this chapter is to untangle the intricate tapestry of experiences and nuances that define each type. Acting as a compass, it serves as a guide to differentiate between various anxiety disorders, providing clarity and understanding to teenagers navigating the complexities of their mental health.

# The Spectrum of Anxiety Disorders

## Complexity of Anxiety Disorders

Commence by recognizing the diverse landscape of anxiety disorders, each presenting a unique set of challenges. Acknowledge that anxiety disorders are not a one-size-fits-all phenomenon; instead, they manifest in various forms, each with distinct characteristics and impacts on daily life.

# <u>Generalized Anxiety Disorder (GAD)</u>

## <u>Excessive Worry</u>

Illuminate the landscape of Generalized Anxiety Disorder, characterized by persistent and excessive worry about various aspects of life. Dive into the daily struggles faced by individuals with GAD, exploring the all-encompassing nature of their concerns that infiltrate thoughts and emotions.

# <u>Physical Manifestations</u>

Discuss the physical manifestations of GAD, such as muscle tension, restlessness, and fatigue. Paint a vivid picture of how anxiety permeates both the mind and body, affecting overall well-being and daily functioning.

# Social Anxiety

Fear of Social Situations: Navigate the intricate realm of Social Anxiety, marked by an intense fear of social situations. Explore the challenges individuals face when interacting with others, emphasizing the impact on relationships, academic settings, and overall social well-being.

# Overcoming Isolation

Shed light on the isolating nature of social anxiety and the importance of fostering understanding and empathy. Offer insights into building supportive environments that encourage social connection and growth, emphasizing the value of shared experiences.

# Panic Disorder

Sudden and Intense Episodes: Unveil the dynamics of Panic Disorder, characterized by sudden and intense episodes of fear. Explore the visceral experience of panic attacks, detailing the emotional and physical components that define these episodes.

Coping Strategies: Provide practical coping strategies for managing panic attacks, empowering readers to navigate moments of intense anxiety. Discuss the role of mindfulness, breathing exercises, and seeking support during such episodes, emphasizing the importance of a personalized toolkit.

## Other Anxiety Disorders

Specific Phobias: Explore specific phobias, uncovering how intense fears related to specific objects or situations can significantly impact daily life. Discuss the importance of gradual exposure therapy and therapeutic interventions in managing phobias, promoting a step-by-step approach to overcoming fears.

## Obsessive-Compulsive Disorder (OCD)

Delve into the intricate world of OCD, characterized by persistent and intrusive thoughts (obsessions) and repetitive behaviours or mental acts (compulsions). Illuminate the challenges individuals face in managing these obsessions and compulsions, emphasizing the role of therapeutic interventions and support.

# Post-Traumatic Stress Disorder (PTSD)

Navigate the landscape of PTSD, often stemming from traumatic experiences. Discuss the range of symptoms, from flashbacks to hypervigilance, and emphasize the importance of trauma-informed care, recognizing the resilience and strength required in the healing process.

# Distinguishing Features

## Overlapping Themes

Discuss the potential for comorbidity, where

individuals may experience more than one anxiety

disorder simultaneously. Explore the overlapping

themes and shared challenges, fostering an

understanding of the interconnected nature of

anxiety disorders. Emphasize the importance of a

holistic approach to mental health, considering the

multifaceted aspects of an individual's experience.

By the chapter's conclusion, readers should

emerge with a nuanced understanding of the

spectrum of anxiety disorders. The goal is to empower teenagers to recognize and differentiate between various types of anxiety disorders, fostering empathy and creating a foundation for informed discussions about mental health. The tone throughout should be informative, compassionate, and geared towards dispelling myths and stereotypes surrounding anxiety disorders.

## Impact on Daily Life

# Chapter 4

## Impact on Daily Life

## Navigating Challenges with Resilience

In this chapter, we embark on a journey to unravel the profound ways in which anxiety can permeate and influence daily life. Our exploration encompasses its effects on activities, relationships, and school performance, with a focus on recognizing the signs and symptoms through this understanding, readers will gain insight into the intricate dance between anxiety and the various facets of their lives, empowering them to navigate these challenges with resilience.

## Influence on Daily Activities

## Interference with Routine

Anxiety, at its peak, has the potential to disrupt daily activities and routines. Explore the challenges individuals face when anxiety becomes a formidable barrier to completing tasks, making decisions, or engaging in activities they once found joy in.

# Impact on Productivity

Delve into the relationship between anxiety and productivity, shedding light on how persistent worries and fears can hinder one's ability to focus and accomplish goals. Discuss the cyclical nature of anxiety, where the fear of the future may lead to a sense of being overwhelmed in the present.

## Strain on Relationships

## Interpersonal Dynamics

Navigate the complexities of how anxiety can strain interpersonal relationships. Discuss the challenges faced in expressing oneself, forming connections and maintaining healthy relationships when anxiety becomes a constant companion.

## Communication Barriers

Illuminate the potential communication barriers that arise when anxiety takes centre stage. Discuss how misunderstandings, fear of judgment, or difficulty expressing emotions may impact the quality of relationships with family, friends, and peers.

## Academic Performance

Impact on Concentration: Anxiety poses significant challenges to concentration and focus on an academic setting. Explore how persistent worries about performance, exams, and social interactions can create mental hurdles, hindering a student's ability to engage fully in their studies.

## Test Anxiety

Delve into the phenomenon of test anxiety, where the fear of exams can manifest physically and emotionally, impacting performance. Offer practical strategies for managing test anxiety, emphasizing the importance of a positive mindset towards academic challenges.

# Recognizing Signs and Symptoms

Behavioural Indicators: Provide insight into the behavioural signs that may indicate the presence of anxiety. This includes changes in sleep patterns, appetite, and avoidance behaviours. Empower readers to recognize these indicators in themselves or others, fostering early detection and intervention.

Emotional Telltale Signs: Explore the emotional dimensions of anxiety, such as persistent worry, irritability, and feelings of restlessness. By understanding the emotional landscape, individuals can gain insight into their mental well-being, laying the foundation for self-awareness and proactive mental health management.

Physical Manifestations: Shed light on the physical manifestations of anxiety, encompassing symptoms like muscle tension, headaches, and gastrointestinal issues. Recognizing the interconnected nature of physical and mental health aids in early detection, emphasizing the holistic approach required for comprehensive well-being.

# Chapter 5

## Coping Mechanisms and Self-Help

## Nurturing Inner Strength

In this pivotal chapter, we embark on a journey into the realm of coping mechanisms and self-help strategies, providing practical tools to empower teenagers in managing anxiety on a daily basis. By delving into techniques such as breathing exercises, mindfulness, and positive affirmations, readers will discover a repertoire of methods to nurture their inner strength and resilience.

# Breathing Exercises

## The Power of Breath

Illuminate the transformative power of conscious breathing in managing anxiety. Introduce readers to various breathing exercises, such as diaphragmatic breathing and square breathing, providing step-by-step instructions to foster a sense of calm and relaxation.

In-the-Moment Techniques: Offer breathing techniques that can be employed in-the-moment when anxiety arises. Emphasize the accessibility and effectiveness of breathwork in regulating the nervous system and promoting a grounded state of mind.

## Mindfulness Practices

Foundations of Mindfulness: Introduce the concept of mindfulness as a foundational practice for anxiety management. Explore the benefits of staying present, acknowledging thoughts without judgment, and cultivating awareness of the present moment.

## Mindful Activities

Provide a range of mindful activities that can be easily incorporated into daily life. This may include mindful breathing, mindful walking, and mindful eating, encouraging readers to infuse mindfulness into various aspects of their routine.

## Positive Affirmations

Harnessing Positive Energy: Explore the power of positive affirmations in shifting thought patterns and promoting a positive mindset. Guide readers in creating personalized affirmations that resonate with their experiences and aspirations.

## Integration into Daily Routine

Discuss practical ways to integrate positive affirmations into daily routines. Whether through morning rituals, sticky notes, or digital reminders,

emphasize the importance of consistent

affirmation practice for mental well-being.

## Journaling for Reflection

## Therapeutic Expression

Introduce journaling as a therapeutic tool for self-

reflection. Encourage readers to express their

thoughts and emotions on paper, providing an

outlet for processing feelings and gaining insights

into their mental state.

# Gratitude Journaling

Explore the practice of gratitude journaling as a means of cultivating a positive perspective. Guide readers in acknowledging and recording moments of gratitude, fostering a mindset shift towards appreciation.

## stablishing Healthy Habits

## Sleep Hygiene

Emphasize the crucial role of sleep-in mental well-being. Provide tips for establishing healthy sleep hygiene, including consistent sleep schedules, minimizing screen time before bed, and creating a restful sleep environment.

## Physical Activity

Highlight the positive impact of regular physical activity on mental health. Encourage readers to find activities they enjoy, whether it's yoga, walking, or team sports, as a means of releasing built-up tension and boosting mood.

## Seeking Professional Support

# Importance of Professional Help

Acknowledge that self-help strategies are valuable, but seeking professional support is equally crucial. Destigmatize therapy and counselling, emphasizing that trained professionals can provide tailored guidance and support.

## Available Resources

Provide information on accessing mental health resources, including school counsellors, therapists, and helplines. Empower readers to reach out for help when needed, fostering a proactive approach to mental health care.

By the chapter's end, readers should feel equipped with a toolkit of coping mechanisms and self-help strategies to navigate the complexities of anxiety. The overarching goal is to empower teenagers with practical, accessible tools that can be integrated into their daily lives, fostering resilience and promoting a proactive approach to mental well-being. The tone should be supportive, encouraging, and geared towards instilling a sense of agency in managing anxiety through personalized self-help practices

Medication for Anxiety

# Chapter 6

## Medication for Anxiety

## Navigating Treatment Options

In this pivotal chapter, we embark on a comprehensive exploration of medication for anxiety, providing readers with valuable insights into common prescriptions, their advantages, and potential side effects. By offering an in-depth understanding of medication as a treatment option, we empower readers to confidently navigate the complexities of managing their anxiety.

## Understanding Medication for Anxiety

## Role of Medication

The role of medication in managing anxiety is illuminated, emphasizing its position among various treatment options. This chapter delves into the significance of personalized treatment plans, underscoring how medication can complement other therapeutic approaches. By understanding the nuanced role of medication, readers are empowered to make informed choices tailored to their individual needs. The collaborative nature of treatment decisions is highlighted, fostering a sense of agency in the readers' mental health journey.

## Neurotransmitter Regulation

The intricate workings of anxiety medications in regulating neurotransmitters are explored, with a specific focus on serotonin, dopamine, and gamma-aminobutyric acid (GABA). Complex concepts are simplified to ensure readers grasp the fundamental mechanisms, providing them with a solid foundation to comprehend how these medications affect brain chemistry. This understanding serves as a crucial tool for readers in evaluating the potential impact of medications on their anxiety.

## Commonly Prescribed Medications

Selective Serotonin Reuptake Inhibitors (SSRIs)

SSRIs are introduced as a commonly prescribed class of medications for anxiety. The chapter delves into how SSRIs enhance serotonin levels in the brain, effectively addressing symptoms of anxiety. Specific SSRIs are highlighted, offering readers insights into the benefits associated with each. This information enables readers to make informed decisions about the potential medications that align with their unique needs.

## Benzodiazepines

The use of benzodiazepines for acute anxiety relief is explored, emphasizing their fast-acting nature. Potential drawbacks, including the risk of dependence and withdrawal symptoms, are discussed with a focus on promoting cautious and short-term usage for optimal outcomes. This section aims to provide readers with a balanced understanding of the benefits and potential risks associated with benzodiazepines.

## Serotonin-Norepinephrine Reuptake Inhibitors (SNRIs)

**SNRIs** are introduced as medications targeting both serotonin and norepinephrine. The chapter delves into their efficacy in treating anxiety disorders, providing readers with an understanding of potential side effects and benefits associated with this class of medications. By presenting this information, readers are equipped to consider the diverse options available and make decisions aligned with their preferences

and concerns.

## Benefits of Anxiety Medication

## Symptom Reduction

The positive impact of anxiety medication on

symptom reduction is highlighted, addressing

excessive worry, panic attacks, and physical

manifestations of anxiety. Readers gain insights

into how medication can enhance daily

functioning and contribute to overall well-being.

This section aims to instil confidence in readers

about the tangible benefits that medication can bring to their lives.

## Improved Quality of Life

The chapter explores how medication may contribute to an improved quality of life by enabling individuals to engage more fully in activities, relationships, and academic pursuits. Emphasis is placed on the potential for enhanced overall functioning and a more fulfilling life. Readers are encouraged to envision the positive changes medication could bring, promoting a hopeful outlook.

# Potential Side Effects and Considerations

## Common Side Effects

Potential side effects associated with anxiety medication, such as nausea, drowsiness, and changes in appetite, are discussed. Reassurance is provided, emphasizing that these side effects are often temporary and can be effectively managed. This information aims to alleviate concerns and empower readers to navigate potential side effects proactively.

## Long-Term Considerations

Concerns about long-term use, dependency, and withdrawal symptoms are addressed. The importance of close monitoring by healthcare professionals and the gradual tapering of medications when discontinuation is appropriate are emphasized to alleviate reader concerns. By addressing long-term considerations, readers are encouraged to approach medication with a well-informed and balanced perspective.

## Individualized Treatment Plans

# Collaborative Decision-Making

The chapter stresses the importance of collaborative decision-making between individuals and healthcare providers. Readers are encouraged to engage in open communication about concerns, preferences, and treatment goals to tailor medication plans to their unique needs. This collaborative approach fosters a sense of partnership between individuals and their healthcare providers, enhancing the efficacy of treatment.

# Combination Approaches

The potential benefits of a combination of medication and psychotherapy are discussed, highlighting the synergistic effects of these approaches in addressing the multifaceted nature of anxiety. Readers are informed about the flexibility of treatment plans to suit evolving needs. This section encourages readers to consider a holistic approach, recognizing the value of combining medication with psychotherapeutic interventions for comprehensive care.

## Monitoring and Adjustments

# Regular Check-Ins

The necessity of regular check-ins with healthcare providers to monitor medication efficacy and potential side effects is emphasized. Readers are encouraged to actively communicate any changes in their condition to ensure optimal outcomes. Regular check-ins are presented as a proactive measure, promoting ongoing collaboration between individuals and their healthcare providers.

## Adjustments as Needed

The possibility of medication adjustments based on individual response and changing circumstances is discussed. Reassurance is provided, conveying that treatment plans are flexible and can be adapted to suit evolving needs, promoting a sense of agency in the readers' mental health journey. This section empowers readers to actively participate in their treatment, recognizing that adjustments are a natural part of the process.

By the end of this chapter, readers are equipped with a comprehensive understanding of medication for anxiety, enabling them to make informed decisions about their mental health care.

The tone throughout is informative, reassuring, and focused on fostering a sense of agency in navigating treatment options for anxiety. This chapter serves as a valuable resource for individuals seeking clarity and guidance on their journey towards better mental health.

# Support from Friends and Family

# Chapter 7

# Support from Friends and Family

## Allies in Managing Anxiety

In this pivotal chapter, we delve into the profound impact that friends and family can have as invaluable allies in the journey of managing anxiety. By emphasizing the crucial elements of open communication and empathy, readers will gain valuable insights into cultivating a supportive network that significantly contributes to their mental well-being.

## The Role of Friends and Family

## Essential Pillars

Friends and family serve as essential pillars of

support in the multifaceted journey of managing

anxiety. Illuminate the unique and irreplaceable

role they play in providing emotional

understanding, practical assistance, and

unwavering support.

## Creating a Supportive Environment

Discuss the significance of establishing a nurturing and supportive environment both at home and within friend circles. Explore the positive ripple effects of such an atmosphere on overall mental health and well-being.

## Encouraging Open Communication

## Breaking the Silence

Highlight the importance of breaking the silence surrounding anxiety within the family and friend circles. Discuss the potential benefits of fostering an atmosphere of open and honest conversations about mental health, creating a space for vulnerability, and understanding.

## Active Listening

Introduce the concept of active listening as a foundational element of effective communication. Provide practical guidance on how friends and family can engage in active listening without judgment, fostering a safe and empathetic space for expression.

# Building Empathy and Understanding

## Educating Loved Ones

Discuss the pivotal role of education in building empathy among friends and family. Provide accessible resources and information to help them better understand anxiety disorders, dispelling myths, and contributing to the reduction of stigma.

Empathy in Action: Illustrate tangible ways in which friends and family can express empathy. Explore the transformative power of validating emotions, offering reassurance, and simply being present for their loved ones experiencing anxiety.

# Providing Practical Support

## Assistance with Daily Tasks

Explore the ways in which friends and family can provide practical support in daily tasks, effectively alleviating some of the stress associated with anxiety. Discuss the importance of collaborative efforts in managing responsibilities.

## Accompanying to Appointments

Highlight the significance of accompanying individuals to therapy or medical appointments. Discuss the instrumental role of emotional support during these critical moments, emphasizing the

strength derived from shared experiences.

## Recognizing Boundaries

## Respecting Personal Space

Discuss the importance of respecting personal

boundaries when supporting someone with

anxiety. Explore the delicate balance between

offering assistance and allowing space for

individual coping mechanisms, fostering a sense of

autonomy.

# Encouraging Independence

Empower friends and family to encourage independence in managing anxiety. Discuss the value of fostering self-reliance while maintaining a supportive presence, acknowledging the individual's agency in their mental health journey.

## Nurturing Healthy Relationships

## Strengthening Connections

Explore how supportive relationships contribute significantly to mental well-being. Discuss the reciprocal nature of healthy relationships and how they can act as a protective factor against anxiety, fostering a sense of security and trust.

## Seeking Professional Guidance

Highlight the pivotal role of friends and family in encouraging their loved ones to seek professional guidance when needed. Emphasize that professional support complements and enhances the existing support network, contributing to comprehensive mental health care.

By the conclusion of this chapter, readers should not only recognize but deeply appreciate the pivotal role that friends and family play in managing anxiety. The overarching goal is to empower both individuals dealing with anxiety and their support network to actively cultivate an environment characterized by understanding, empathy, and open communication. The tone should remain supportive, informative, and focused on fostering strong connections within the support system.

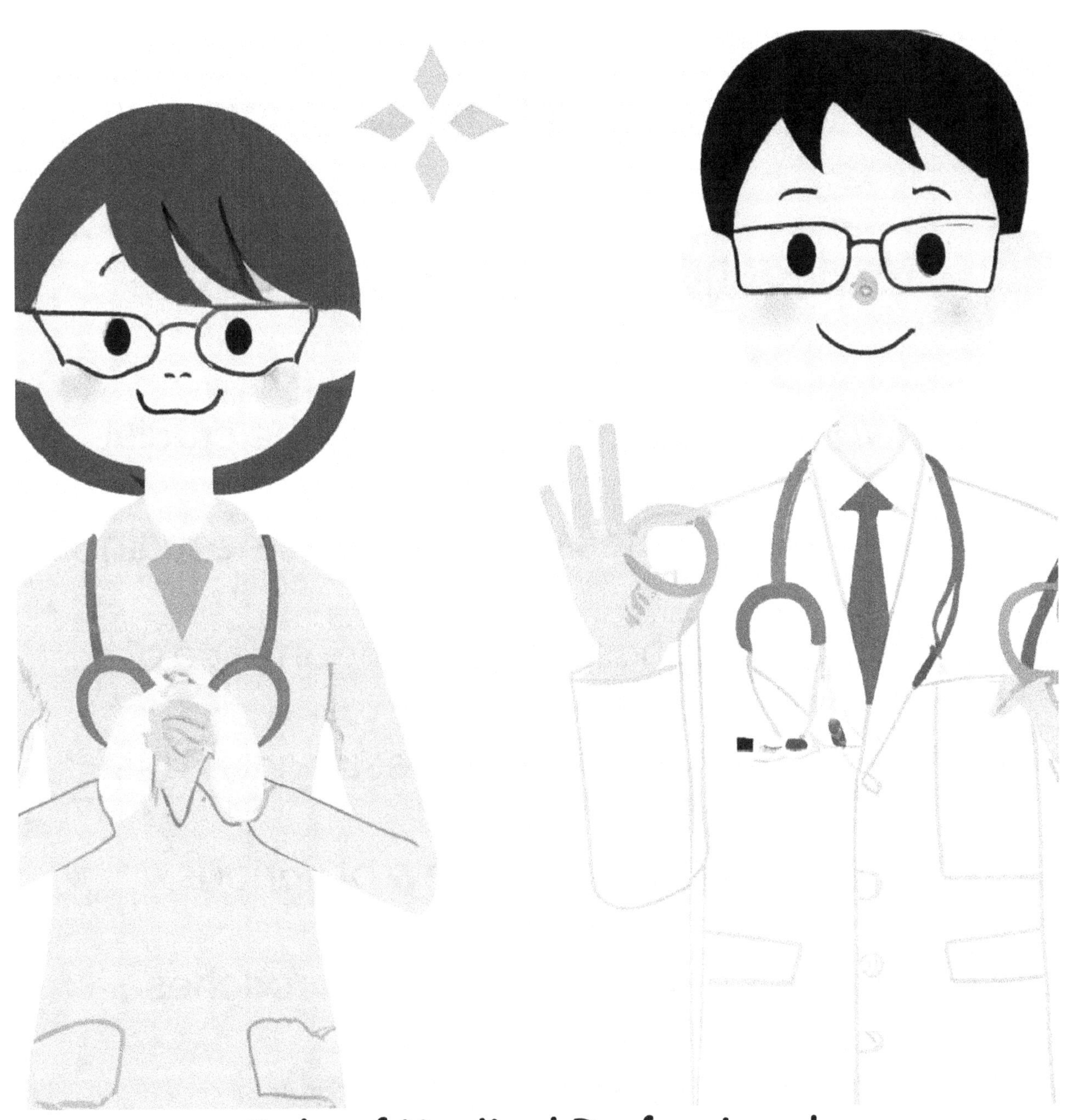

# Role of Medical Professionals

# Chapter 8

## Role of Medical Professionals

## Navigating Mental Health Support

In this pivotal chapter, we delve into the crucial role that medical professionals play in the realm of mental health, emphasizing the importance of seeking help from qualified professionals. This exploration includes an overview of various therapy options and counselling approaches available for individuals navigating the complexities of anxiety.

# Understanding the Importance of Seeking Help

## Professional Expertise

Illuminate the invaluable expertise that mental health professionals bring to the table. Emphasize the specialized training and knowledge they possess in understanding and treating various mental health concerns, particularly anxiety disorders.

# Breaking Stigmas

Discuss the importance of breaking stigmas surrounding seeking professional help for mental health issues. Foster an understanding that reaching out to professionals is a proactive step towards well-being and an integral part of self-care.

# Overview of Therapy Options

## Individual Therapy (Counselling)

Provide an in-depth overview of individual therapy, commonly known as counselling. Explore the one-on-one dynamic between the individual and the therapist, highlighting the confidential and supportive nature of this therapeutic relationship.

## Group Therapy

Introduce the concept of group therapy, emphasizing the power of shared experiences and mutual support. Discuss how group settings can provide a sense of community and understanding, particularly beneficial for individuals dealing with anxiety.

## Cognitive-Behavioural Therapy (CBT)

Explore the principles of Cognitive-Behavioural Therapy, a widely used therapeutic approach for anxiety disorders. Break down how CBT addresses thought patterns and behaviours, empowering individuals to manage and overcome anxiety.

## Mindfulness-Based Therapies

Discuss the growing popularity of mindfulness-based therapies, such as Mindfulness-Based Stress Reduction (MBSR) and Mindfulness-Based Cognitive Therapy (MBCT). Illustrate how mindfulness practices can enhance self-awareness and reduce anxiety.

# Counselling Approaches

## Psychodynamic Therapy

Introduce psychodynamic therapy, exploring its emphasis on understanding unconscious processes and early life experiences. Discuss how this approach can contribute to insights into the root causes of anxiety.

## Humanistic Therapy

Highlight the humanistic approach to therapy, focusing on self-exploration, personal growth, and the inherent value of individuals. Discuss how humanistic therapy can empower individuals to take charge of their mental health journey.

## Holistic Counselling

Explore the concept of holistic counselling, which considers the interconnectedness of mental, emotional, and physical well-being. Discuss how holistic approaches can provide a comprehensive understanding and treatment of anxiety.

# Collaborative Decision-Making in Treatment

## Tailoring Treatment Plans

Emphasize the collaborative nature of developing treatment plans with mental health professionals. Discuss the importance of open communication, ensuring that treatment approaches align with individual preferences, goals, and comfort levels.

## Incorporating Medication when Necessary:

Highlight the possibility of incorporating medication into treatment plans when deemed necessary. Discuss the collaborative decision-making process between individuals and mental health professionals regarding the use of

medication for anxiety.

## Overcoming Barriers to Seeking Help

## Addressing Concerns

Acknowledge common concerns and barriers

individuals may face when considering seeking

help. Provide reassurance and information to

address issues such as stigma, fear, or uncertainty

about therapy.

# Promoting Accessibility

Discuss the importance of promoting accessibility to mental health services. Explore resources, such as community clinics, online therapy platforms, and helplines, that can enhance the availability of mental health support.

By the end of this chapter, readers should recognize the pivotal role that medical professionals play in supporting mental health, especially in the context of anxiety. The goal is to empower individuals to seek help, break down stigmas associated with mental health care, and provide a comprehensive understanding of the various therapy options and counselling approaches available. The tone should remain supportive, informative, and focused on encouraging proactive steps towards mental well-being.

<u>Urgent Issues</u>

# Chapter 9

## Urgent Issues

## Suicide Prevention

In this crucial chapter, we delve into the urgent matter of suicide prevention, equipping readers with essential information on identifying warning signs of suicidal thoughts and providing a roadmap of steps to take if someone is in crisis. Recognizing the gravity of this issue, our aim is to empower individuals to play an active role in preventing suicides by understanding the signs

and taking appropriate actions.

## Identifying Warning Signs of Depression

### Behavioural Signs

morbid thoughts may manifest in behaviours such

as withdrawing from social activities, giving away

possessions, or sudden mood changes. By

recognizing these behavioural indicators,

individuals can be more vigilant about the well-

being of those around them.

# Verbal Cues

Verbal expressions of hopelessness, feelings of being trapped, or explicit desires to end one's life should be taken seriously. This section emphasizes the importance of active listening and responding empathetically to verbal cues.

# Emotional Warning Signs

Persistent feelings of sadness, overwhelming guilt, or a sense of worthlessness are emotional warning signs that require attention. Encouraging readers to be attuned to emotional shifts helps in identifying potential risks.

# Steps to Take if Someone is in Crisis

## Immediate Action

This section underscores the urgency of immediate action when someone is in crisis. Staying calm, focused, and promptly addressing the situation is crucial for the individual's safety.

## Engage in Conversation

Guidance on engaging in a non-judgmental and empathetic conversation is provided, emphasizing active listening and expressing concern without passing judgment.

## <u>Encourage Professional Help</u>

Recognizing the importance of professional assistance, readers are encouraged to guide individuals in crisis toward mental health professionals, helplines, or emergency services, with relevant contact information provided.

## <u>Stay with the Person</u>

Highlighting the value of companionship during a crisis, the importance of not leaving the person alone is stressed, accompanied by reassurance of available support.

## Remove Means of Harm

Acknowledging the significance of immediate environmental safety, readers are advised to remove potential means of self-harm or suicide from the person's surroundings.

## Contact Support Networks

Involving the person's support network, such as friends, family, or colleagues, is emphasized for additional assistance and emotional support.

# Follow-Up Support

The section stresses the importance of ongoing support, encouraging readers to maintain communication and assist the individual in connecting with mental health professionals for long-term assistance.

## Promoting Mental Health Awareness

## Education and Awareness

The role of education and awareness in suicide prevention is emphasized, aiming to reduce stigma and create an environment where individuals feel comfortable seeking help.

# Community Resources

Readers are provided with information on community resources, support groups, and initiatives dedicated to suicide prevention, promoting active engagement in a supportive and informed community.

# Self-Care Practices

Recognizing the significance of self-care in maintaining mental well-being, the chapter explores various activities that individuals can incorporate into their routines to manage stress, anxiety, and other mental health challenges.

By the end of this chapter, readers are equipped with valuable insights into recognizing warning signs of suicidal thoughts and taking immediate steps to address a crisis. The tone remains empathetic, supportive, and focuses on encouraging proactive measures in dealing with urgent mental health issues, ultimately fostering a community that is informed and actively engaged in promoting mental health awareness and w

Moving Forward

# Chapter 10

## Moving Forward

## Building Resilience

In this transformative chapter, we embark on a journey toward building resilience—a fundamental aspect of effectively dealing with anxiety. Through the provision of long-term strategies, encouragement of a proactive approach to mental well-being, and promotion of resilience and personal growth, the objective is to empower individuals in navigating life's challenges with strength and adaptability.

## Long-Term Strategies

## for Dealing with Anxiety

## Holistic Well-being

This section underscores the significance of adopting a holistic approach to well-being, integrating physical, mental, and emotional health. Strategies encompassing regular exercise, maintaining a balanced diet, and ensuring sufficient sleep are explored as essential contributors to overall anxiety management.

# Lifestyle Modifications

Delving into the impact of lifestyle choices on anxiety, readers are guided to make positive modifications. This includes effectively managing stressors, establishing realistic goals, and cultivating healthy habits conducive to long-term mental well-being.

# Mindfulness Practices

The chapter delves into mindfulness practices as effective tools for managing anxiety over the long run. Techniques such as meditation, deep breathing exercises, and engaging in mindfulness-based activities are introduced to enhance self-awareness and facilitate stress reduction.

## Encouraging a Proactive Approach to Mental Well-being

Self-Care Rituals: Readers are encouraged to establish personalized self-care rituals, emphasizing activities that bring joy, relaxation, and fulfilment. This section explores the pivotal role of self-care in maintaining mental balance and preventing anxiety.

# Regular Mental Health Check-Ins

Advocating for a proactive stance toward mental well-being, individuals are advised to conduct regular mental health check-ins. Reflective practices, journaling, and seeking professional support when needed are discussed as integral components of self-awareness.

## Setting Boundaries

Establishing healthy boundaries emerges as a crucial aspect of mental well-being. This section explores the importance of setting limits on commitments, managing expectations, and recognizing when to say no as part of a proactive approach to prevent overwhelming stress.

## Promoting Resilience and Personal Growth

### Resilience Building

The chapter introduces the concept of resilience and its pivotal role in bouncing back from challenges. Readers are guided through exercises and mindset shifts contributing to building resilience, emphasizing adaptability and strength in the face of adversity.

# Learning from Adversity

Highlighting the potential for personal growth through adversity, this section encourages individuals to view challenges as opportunities for learning and development. Strategies for reframing perspectives and finding meaning in difficult experiences are discussed.

# Seeking Professional Development

Promoting personal growth, readers are encouraged to seek professional development opportunities. This may include pursuing education, acquiring new skills, or engaging in activities that align with individual passions and aspirations.

By the chapter's conclusion, readers are armed with effective long-term strategies for managing anxiety, motivated to adopt a proactive approach to mental well-being, and inspired to foster resilience and personal growth. The tone maintains a positive and empowering stance, aiming to instil a mindset that embraces challenges as catalysts for profound growth and transformation.